VICTORIAN VOICES

In memory of my father,
Hartley Thwaite

VICTORIAN VOICES

ANTHONY THWAITE

Oxford New York Toronto Melbourne

OXFORD UNIVERSITY PRESS

1980

Oxford University Press, Walton Street, Oxford OX2 6DP

London Glasgow New York Toronto
Delhi Bombay Calcutta Madras Karachi
Kuala Lumpur Singapore Hong Kong Tokyo
Nairobi Dar es Salaam Cape Town
Melbourne Wellington

and associate companies in
Beirut Berlin Ibadan Mexico City

British Library Cataloguing in Publication Data

Thwaite, Anthony
Victorian voices.
I. Title
821'.9'14   PR6070.H9V| 80-40296
ISBN 0-19-211937-0

Printed in Great Britain by
The Bowering Press Limited
Plymouth

Contents

Acknowledgements

Some of these poems have been broadcast by the BBC and published in *Ambit, Encounter, London Magazine, New Review, New Statesman, Thames Poetry, The Times Literary Supplement*, and the *Poetry Book Society Christmas Supplement* 1979.

1 At Marychurch

Here at the bench in front of me, the flasks
Ripple and throb with all the simulacra
Providence has provided; the various tasks
Assigned to each and all by their Creator
Perform and are performed. Forests of spines,
Vitals enclosed in hollow boxes, shells
Built of a thousand pieces, glide along
Majestically over rock and reef.
Yonder a *Medusa* goes, pumping its sluggish way
Laboriously, not ineffectually,
Beneath the surface of the clear wave;
A mass of *Millepore*, a honeycomb
Much like the second stomach of an Ox,
Slimes, reappears, retires, appears once more;
And there, that massive shrub of stone, the coy
Calcareous atoms of the *Madrepore*,
Short branches, branched and branched again, pierced through
With holes innumerable, threaded with tentacles.
Ha! Here is the little architect
Ready to answer for himself; he thrusts his head
And shoulders from his chimney-top, and shouts
His cognomen of *Melicerta ringens*.
Look! He is in the very act of building
Now. Did you see him suddenly
Bow down his head and lay a brick upon
The top of the last course? And now again
He builds another brick; his mould a tiny cup
Below his chin, his sole material
The floating floccose atoms of his refuse. So
Prochronically pellets build to bricks,
Eggs from their chambers, sharks from embryos,
The hollow cones that are the present teeth
Of crocodiles, the tusks of elephants
Refined through layer after layer until
Centuries are accomplished year by year –
And then, after the pulpy fibrous doors

Knocked on in the vegetable world,
The lower tribes, the higher forms – then Man,
Our first progenitor, the primal Head.
What shall we say, we who are chyle and lymph,
Blood, lungs, nails, hair, bones, teeth, phenomena
In the condition of the skeleton
Distinct, the navel corrugated here . . .?
I ask you this: could God have máde these plants,
These animals, this creature that is Man,
Without these retrospective marks? I tell you, no!
A Tree-form without scars limned on its trunk!
A Palm without leaf-bases! Or a Bean
Without a hilum! No laminae
Upon the Tortoise plates! A Carp without
Concentric lines on scales! A Bird that lacks
Feathers! A Mammal without hairs,
Or claws, or teeth, or bones, or blood! A Foetus
With no placenta! In vain, in vain,
These pages, and these ages, if you admit
Such possibilities. That God came down
And made each each, and separately, and whole,
Is manifest in these. Let us suppose
That this, the present year, had been the special
Particular epoch in world history
God had selected as the true beginning,
At his behest, his fiat – what would be
Its state at this Creation? *What exists*
Would still appear precisely as it does.
There would be cities filled with swarms of men;
Houses half-built; castles in ruins; pictures
On artists' easels just sketched in; half-worn
Garments in wardrobes; ships upon the sea;
Marks of birds' footsteps on the mud; the sands
Whitening with skeletons; and human bodies
In burial grounds in stages of decay.
These, and all else, the past, would be found now
Because they are found in the world now, the present age,
Inseparable from the irruption, the one moment

Chosen, the constitution, the condition:
They make it what it has been, will be, is.

The flasks ripple, subside. I am tired. And miles away
I know who sits and writes and tests and proves
Quite other things and other worlds. I fix
My microscope on *Case-fly* and on *Julus*,
The field left clear and undisputed for
The single witness on this other side,
Whose testimony lies before me now:
'In Six Days God Made Heaven and Earth, the Sea,
And All that In Them Is.' Amen. Amen.

2 *A Literary Life*

I tried to open up so many eyes
To the great minds of all humanity.

I thought he liked me, thought I knew him well,
Twin strugglers through the London labyrinth,
Scribblers who learnt the scribbling trade with care –
Though he was never 'Varsity, of course:
How he arrived is something he keeps dark.
A Third in Mods, Second in Law and History,
Is all I have to boast of, but it was
Balliol, with Lang and Mallock, Nettleship,
Prothero, Milner, Rawnsley, Asquith, Cluer . . .
And then my disinheritance (that uncle and his schemes
Of 'business', and my Battels and my cheques,
And mischief in the breach, and no more cheques) –
Well, 'coaching' might have kept me, scraps of Greek
Shoved down the throats of ninnyish nincompoops;
But on that day I strayed into St Giles,
Facing the lectern, opening up the book,
Placing my finger with unopened eyes –
Those words (Acts Nine, Verse Six): 'Arise and go
Into the city, and it shall be told thee
What thou must do.' Nothing in view, alone,
Without inheritance, and penniless,
I came to London.

                              December Seventy-two –
The 'turnover', my first, a causerie
Of thoughts on 'End of Term' – oh guineas earned
Deliriously, scribbling eight hours a day
Fusty and musty in a dear old garret
Off Temple Bar, addressing envelopes
For half a crown per thousand for the *Globe*;
Letters from Swinburne about Tourneur ('if you should
Run up here sometime may I have the pleasure
Of seeing you in these rooms . . .' – the very words!)

So I aimed high, and higher, up and up –
With Leslie Stephen in the *Cornhill*, Smith
Taking my 'Dryden' for the *Quarterly*,
And work, and work, and work . . . I must jot down this:
That evening, out at Putney, A.C.S.
Invited me to hear him read his new
Volume of poems. Dobson, O'Shaughnessy, Watts,
William Rossetti, Marston – The Pines was full
Of singing birds, and I among them all.
What bliss to see them, hear them, watch the frail
Outlandish Swinburne leap and shriek and moan
Immortal verses! But it could not last.
Another year or so, and we fell out.

Extension Lectures down at Brixton, Richmond
(Frequently honoured by the Princess May,
Later to be our Queen, Duchess of Teck,
And other notables), Hackney (in Lent
Of Ninety-one, 'The poetry of Browning'),
Anerley, Ascot, Balham, Battersea,
Crouch End and Cheshunt, Highbury and Lee –
An interview with Browning, one with Froude,
And then, and then – the Chair at Birmingham . . .

But nothing quite right yet: others made way,
Climbed ladders, set their mark, were darlings all
Of quarterlies and salons and the most
Important colleges – such as my long-time friend,
Or so I thought him, one-time, some-time friend
Who gave those Cambridge lectures – tall and sleek
And full of names dropped, fudge upon the page,
And errors, errors, errors by the ton.
To say so in the *Quarterly Review*
Was – surely? – a good office, what a straight
Purposive fellow ought to say, in truth:
No personal attack – here was a book
(All pasted up for lectures) which was gross
With slovenly facts, deplorable and low . . .

5

But that I said so – this was beyond the pale,
Though Gladstone, Huxley, Arnold, took my point:
I think they did . . . The truth is hard to find.
What lodges in my skull is that fine phrase
They say the Laureate uttered to my friend
(My one-time friend) – 'You want to hear my view
Of that man J.C.C.? I tell you this –
A louse upon the locks of literature!'

After that, Birmingham, books, and Conan Doyle,
A touch of the old trouble – a low state
Of worn depression, sometimes several days –
And finally, the School of Journalism
To be my final crown . . .

Well, there it was, and here I am, a man
More sinned against than sinning, waking up
At ten to ten in Lowestoft, and going
Out for a walk a little dizzily
(A sleeping draught perhaps), and stepping in
To four foot six of water and thick mud.

Among the many papers found on me
A stained sheet with some careful jottings made
For the forthcoming Johnson Celebrations,
And these words too, which need no note or gloss:
'Poems in couplets written so that each
Couplet has two or three emphatic syllables,
Two or one in the first line, one in the second
Commencing with the same – this is also
The initial of the chief emphatic syllable
In the second line: thus, "I was wearie of wandering
And went me to reste
Under a brod banke
Bi a bourne side".'

And scholarship, and literature, live on:
As once I heeded, heedless others stray
Ennobled in their errors. Here I lie.

6

3 To a Girl of the Period

Will the bent bow spring back, the strained cord break?
Will temperament and long usage prove too strong?
But three months married, and I ask how long
All this will last . . . Before him, other men
Seemed apt to take me gladly: I refused,
Notoriously unanchored, a free woman
Convinced that all society is built up
By process of experiment, that the last
Word has not been said on anything.
These were the very phrases that I used,
Intent to build the future with a past
Weighed, sieved, rejected if the test so proved.

*

And was it then for pity that I loved,
Or thought I loved? Those boys and girls of his,
Quaint scoffed-at relics, an eccentric's toys –
All dressed in coarse blue flannel, Nazarenes
With love-locks to their shoulders, picturesque
As Botticelli's angels. One forgave
Thoughts of unfitness for their beauty's sake –
And so their father: his face the face of Christ,
Believing revolution was at hand,
When wars would cease, when justice without flaw
And abstract right would swiftly take the place
Of mere expedience, when the reign of peace
And truth and purity of life – alike
For men and women – would begin at last.

So I have walked the wood, and have picked up
The crooked stick. But wherein lay the flaw,
As it still lies? For he was sweet in word,
His manner acquiescent, and he smiled
To be compliant – indeed, did much I wished
Because I wished it. But I never touched

7

The core. The shortcomings, the weaknesses,
Lay all about. The intimacy of marriage
Forced them upon me.

                    We kept open house -
But open to our opposites: round him,
Poor patriots and penniless propagandists,
While those whom I invited he pronounced
'Worldly, ungodly, frivolous, fashionable'.
For him, my taste in proper sense of dress
(Off with the children's medieval rags
And on with frocks for girls, jackets for boys)
Was dandyism, forethought was faithlessness,
Conventional propriety just 'fashion'.

Was it my money ruined us, dependence
Of the traditional breadwinner on one
Who added to her faults of practical rigour
The graver fault of riches? His engraving
Brought in its fees, but was precarious.
The burden of the children and the home
Fell to my energies, while Utopia
Took all his time. Clean linen tablecloths,
The accurate adding-up of butchers' bills,
Were trivial stuff to him – and to me also,
Yet must be seen to. All my early ardour,
The independence which I sought and won,
Reduced to coaxing, nagging, silences
More terrible than either . . . Well, the parting came,
So gradual that *drifting* is the word
That fits it best.

                  And words are what I have –
Use, now, as my sole weapon – not to call to arms
The Shrieking Sisterhood, Wild Women shrill,
Revolting daughters (as experience
Lived through and suffered might have given me cause),
But to *condemn* them, sexless masks of men,

8

Hard, without love, ambitious, mercenary,
Without domestic faculty and devoid
Of healthy natural instincts . . . So with spitting rage
Women and men attack me, 'Girl of the Period'
Cartooned and comedied and turned to farce,
The hoyden travesty. No one in the world
Honours and loves true women more than I,
But then they must be *women* – with their faults,
But better than the adopted faults of *men*!
Misrepresented and misunderstood,
I pen another article while I know
Its fate is to be twisted, jeered at, burnt,
Mangled for sermons, told it takes a view
Branding a woman no better than a cow . . .

*

Maternity – that blessèd, blessèd word
Fulfilling womankind, its benisons
Denied to me. With scarcely hidden tears
I tell you that this little rush of Fame,
This famous notoriety, is nothing
Compared with that imagined ecstasy
For which I yearned, for which I was so fitted
By temperament, by body, and by skill.
Babes of my reveries, shawled plumply in my arms,
Products of finest art, of care and love,
You must belong to others. Knowing all
In my own person, all that women suffer
When actively they launch into the fray,
I would prevent with all my strength young girls
From following my own unwilled mistakes –
Guard them, indeed, with my own body from
Such insults as my life has given me,
Teach them to be themselves – and to be free.

4 *Messages from Government House*

The Punjab war is done: in all the land
No man in arms against us. Those who bolted
Ran through the Khyber Pass and go on running.
They came like thieves and dash away like thieves.
The Maharajah and the Council signed
Submission yesterday, the British colours
Were hoisted on the Citadel of Lahore,
The Koh-i-noor surrendered to our Queen,
And the Punjab – each inch of it – proclaimed
A portion of our Empire. What I have done
Is my responsibility. I know it
Just, politic, and necessary; my conscience
Tells me the work is one I pray that God
May bless; and with tranquillity I await
My country's sanction and my Queen's approval.
It is not every day an officer
Adds to the British Empire such a prize –
Four million subjects, and the priceless jewel
Of Mogul Emperors to his Sovereign's crown.
This I have done – but do not think that I
Exult unduly: I do not. But when
I feel conviction honestly that this deed
Is for the glory of my land, the honour
Of her most noble majesty, the good
Of those whom I have brought under her rule,
Fitly I may indulge a sentiment
Of honourable pride. Glory to God
For what has been achieved.

                             Some other matters:
A curious discovery at Rangoon –
Digging an old pagoda to make way
For army barracks, our men came across
Gold images and bracelets, with a scroll
Showing these things were put there by a queen
Five hundred years ago. In all such places

One or more images are found of Buddha:
Our fellows call them 'Tommies'. There are few
Pagodas to be seen without a hole
Made by ingenious Britons in their search
For Tommies. I am sorry to admit –
Accessory after the fact, you know –
I purchased secretly myself some bits
Of this mythology when first I reached
Burmah.

   I have a sad death to report –
Bold as his sword, high-minded, kindly, pure,
Devoted to his calling, Mountain is gone.
A Christian soldier, died as he lived. He rests
In the old cemetery at Futteghur.
His widow's on her way here; he'll go home
By the next steamer.

    I have just received
A packet of the rhododendron seeds
Despatched from Kooloo, which the Duchess wished,
And trust they will do well.

     The troops have driven
Moung Goung Gyee out of the Irawaddi:
They took him in the jungle – took his gong,
His gold umbrella and his wife. A pity
The man himself escaped. The place is quiet.

From Barrackpore to Simla, from Peshawar
To Kunawar and Chini, from the camp
At Umritsur to Attok, there is peace.
The reinforcements from Madras have come,
So now I calculate 14,000 men
(5,000 Europeans) are there, thirteen
Steamers upon the river, besides marines
And many sailors. Opium stands high –
On each *per mensem* sale the Government

Gains well. The punishment we meted out
To Rani and to Bunnoo is rewarded –
The Rani people whom Sir Colin thrashed
Last May, destroying valley, stoup and roup,
Have just come in with turbans in their hands
Begging forgiveness, offering allegiance,
Submitting to our fortress. Our success
In sowing dissension between tribe and tribe,
'Twixt Mussulman and Sikh, Hindoo and all,
Is clear: suspicion reigns, and union
Is hopeless between any. Peace and plenty!

*

Just as the office mail was going out,
A rising in Bengal among the hills –
Barbarous folk, though usually timid,
Armed just with bows and arrows: some say greed,
Some say fanaticism, some ill-treatment
By those who build the railway. Troops are there
And closing in. The trouble has not spread
And soon should be put down. But what vexation
Just at the close of my career . . .

*

Before I lay this sceptre down, I plan
To show the court in a most frank despatch
What has been done in India these eight years –
And left undone. I look things in the face.
'Opus exegi': taking leave of those
I ruled over, tomorrow I embark.
The Friend of India some months ago
Called me 'not personally popular'.
If that is true – 'tis not for me to say –
Never were full and copious tears so shed
Over a man *unpopular*, wiped away
By bearded men . . .

                                    I am quite done; my leg
Gives pain continually. Let Canning do
The best he can: the brightest jewel of all
In our imperial crown weighs heavily.
Less easy every day the burden lies –
Annex one province, two others will rise up
Like hydra-headed monsters, their partition
A parturition. What will be born of this?
Rumours and panics and religious wrath
At a few cartridges . . . and 'hope deferred'
At Delhi, given time, indeed one day
'Makes the heart sick' in England. Blow away
The rebels from our cannons, still there hangs
A cloud of blood above the hills and vales,
Ganges, and Indus, and my lost domains.

5 Parables from Nature

Alfred is visiting the Misses Trigg,
Devout old souls whose thread is almost cut;
The girls are at their tasks; and so am I,
A careful mother whose peculiar care's
An infant's pure delight in little things.

O Observation – though restricted now
To Ecclesfield, this room, these walls, this bed –
How I have used you, for diviner use!

In parables and emblems all things spell
Lessons for all of us – my humble gift.
Every true story of humanity
Contains a moral, wrapped and neatly tied
Like an unopened parcel for a child.
We are all children in the eyes of God.
The Crab, the Starfish, and the Bird of night,
The valiant Oak, the Robin Redbreast – all
Teach the inquiring infant to accept
Things as they are, in equanimity.
Red Snow, they say, that falls upon the Alps
(Though I have never ventured from these shores)
Or Great Sea Tangle such as Columbus saw –
Of these I am cognisant, but am more inclined
To nearer things, to close domestic signs.
See how the Bee plunges within the cup,
Fretting its legs with nectar, golden dust,
Always industrious, sweetly employed.
The Long-tailed Tit (*Parus Caudatus*), I chose
After a passage by the Reverend Johns
(*British Birds in their Haunts*) – a happy choice
To illustrate 'the happy family':
For from the moment that a young brood·leaves
The nest until next mating season comes,
Papa, Mama and children keep together
In perfect harmony – the same tree-clump

14

Is their society, they choose together
The next place they shall flit, no one disposed
To stay when all depart, molesting no one,
And suffering, as far as one can see,
No persecution. Here is a pattern made
For all young hands to copy.

                                    It is true
Nature has crueller ways: the House Spider,
Having secured her web, constructs below
Hidden from view a silk apartment whence
Threads are extended, forming a cunning bridge
To the rayed centre – out, then, rushes she
Like a small thunderbolt, seizing her prey with fangs
Which suck the victim dry of all its juices
And then casts out the skeleton-remains!
I do not dwell on that. The value of hair
As a manure for rose-trees was told me
By a prizewinning gentleman who gave
Credit for his success to this device:
Dig in a sheltered place, go pretty deep,
Place in the hole a bone or two, some hair,
Water with soap-suds – practical advice,
And interesting too, to indicate
Animal assisting vegetable,
As vegetable does likewise in its turn.
Nothing can be more satisfactory
As to results. Neither our confidence
Nor yet our comfort are misplaced; no fear
Of being taken in; in all such matters
We are not at chance's mercy; everything
Goes on with regularity, by rules,
By habit; or, as naturalists word it,
By virtue of some *Law*, firm, definite,
A stringent fixity, the Light of Truth.
It is a will on which we can rely;
From past expressions of it, we presume
The future; so we rightfully say *Law*.

The Dragon-fly Grub – a creature whose appearance
Is most unprepossessing, and whose character
Is hardly amiable – can be kept
Happily in a foot-pan filled with water
And fed from ponds or ditches with live insects.
Observe at leisure Metamorphosis –
How, at the chosen moment, this vile thing
Climbs up the Flag or Iris planted there
For your experiment – a rent appears
Within the Pupa case, the wings expand,
And the winged tyrant of the airy world
Most beautifully ascends.

                     O read the book
God's servant, Nature, puts within your ken!
There in these works which seem to puzzle reason
Something divine is hidden, to be discovered
By patient scrutiny. Thus, crickets sing
Loudly, and most troublingly by day,
In damp conditions – as in a cottage here
Where a young mother died by slow degrees
Of a consumption; and it seemed as though
The crickets heralded the sad event.
See on my sun-dial the words I chose,
Hallowed by constant observation – 'Watch,
For ye know not the hour . . .'

                     Now, Juliana,
The day's dictation's finished. Kindly copy
My words in your fair hand. My own, disabled,
Aching and helpless, must lie here unused
Upon the counterpane. I have employment,
I see the sun, love life. And when you pray,
Pray not that I may have less pain but that
More patience may be mine.

6 After High Table

Hockley is turning Papist, so they say:
His set is stiff with incense, and he bobs
Most roguishly in chapel. More and more
The Whore of Babylon extends her sway.
Branston is fiddling with his 'little jobs',
Copying the Bursar's buttery accounts
Into a pocket book he locks away.
In Common Room each night, the floor
Is held by Foxton, face flushed like a plum
About to drop – and we have seen him drop
Drunk as a carter in the smouldering grate.
They are all here, my *Corpus Asinorum*,
Donkeys in orders, stuffed in jowl and crop.
One day it will be said 'He did the state
Some service', when they read my book of fools.

The Master's slack. He does not know the rules.
He is – can't be denied – a natural curate
And would be better suited to the cure
Of souls in Wiltshire, ministering to pigs.
I've seen old Figgins watch him like a ferret,
For Figgins was passed over, and for sure
Preferment went because Enthusiasts
Clamoured for someone without Roman views.
But – pardon me – the Master strokes and frigs
His conscience like a trollop with an itch
Flat on her back and panting in the stews.
All pious mush dressed up as manliness,
Evangelistic canting, keen to bring
Trousers to niggers who don't wear a stitch.
A man's religion is his own. To sing
Barnstorming stanzas to the Lord's as poor
As Newman fluting eunuch fancyings,
His heavenly choir on earth. O that old Whore,
How devious she becomes!

This elm-smoke stings
My eyes at night, when I should be holed up
Snugly behind the bulwark of my oak.
Some more Marsala, or another cup
Of punch . . . What frowsty collared priest is this,
Another chum of Kingston's on the soak
Or snivelling gaitered surrogate from Bath?
Give me your arm – I needs must go and piss.

My colleagues all tread down the primrose path
That – who? – oh, Shakespeare then – put in a play.
I should be even now, I tell you, hard
Pent in my room and working at my book,
Theocritus, my text, my elegiac
Pagan . . .

How these chatterers swill and stay!
I'll take a turn with you around the yard,
The farther quad where dotards never look,
Or if they do, then always back and back
To the dark backward and abysm of time . . .
But then we all are backward-lookers here,
If you would understand me: relicts, men
Who hear the echo when we hear the chime,
As Great Tom stuns the silence. In my ear
I sense the falter of the tolling bell,
I hear it boom again, again, again,
Fetching me back and back, not boding well,
And the full moon hangs high across St Ebbe's . . .

Where was I? Morbid, maybe, at this hour
When Master, Bursar, Chaplain, Dean and all
Waddle like corpulent spiders in their webs
To winding staircases and narrow beds,
To livings without life, posts without power,
A benefice without a benefit.
I have you all marked down . . .

7 The Mentor

Later he wrote: 'On 24th September
Shocked to hear of tragic death of friend
&c': 'keen regret' to him long after
That I and she to whom he was attached
So warmly 'never met or were acquainted
And now would never . . .'

     He was more astute –
Though no less given to subterfuge – than I,
Who saw him first a young, raw, fresh-faced thing.
The 'attachment' that he wrote of was but one
Melded with many others – love-longings
He used as I could not.

     My longings led
Down to the back room of the *Lamb & Flag* –
Brandy-and-water till the dreams took over,
Wafting me back to times when all ran right,
All was about to be, nothing came sour
Against the throat and tongue, nothing looked dark
Against the study-lamp . . . But then the raging,
The boasts and incoherences, the tags
Bellowed or muttered to an audience
That played me for its sport, a thrashing minnow
Swelled to a pike and gorging on the hook.
And, at the last, a brother's troubled arm
Helping me up and out and home to bed,
To toss and twitch and, sweating, sleep it off
Till the next bout would have me in its grip.

The miseries we have become compounded
By those we guess are yet to come, the failings
That magnify to failures. First the sighing
Winds that portend a shower, the scattered drops,
The downpour venting to a steady drizzle
Drenching before and after. So it was:

Small gifts that proved yet smaller, all ambition
Shrunk to a modicum, a way of life.
Workhouse accounts inspected, another novel
Judiciously dissected in review,
A reputation coddled till it smothered.

Onset of autumn – melancholy time
In Cambridge, mists uprising from Coe Fen
Over the causeway, Michaelmas daisies drenched
Drooping their heads in college gardens. Shrouds
Gathered on candles, and foretold a death:
Whose death was supposition – but I knew,
Even as by the mantelpiece I stood
And talked, and heard them guttering; and he
Recognized, too, the sign. And all such signs
Were his to play with, twists and turning points
For fictions, symbols, circumstantial plots . . .

If she I fumbled in hot madness knew
How things had fallen out, our issue growing
Monstrous, strung up as witness of our sin
Though long estranged, the dire inheritance
Of evil warps, repugnant origins,
She would be privy to them. And she knew –
Because she had to bear – the sad beginnings.
I – we – and our son too – we have been used
By one to whom I was mentor . . . yes, and friend:
The dutiful recorder of my trust,
Advice, remonstrance, love. What Homer said,
What Virgil took through labyrinths of metre,
What all my lavished learning broke and spilt,
He bore away, and stored, and deviously
Set out in his inventions. Meanwhile I
Drudged here and there, perpetual ordinand
Not fit to be ordained, my weaknesses
Disguised as scruples or as personal quirks
Familiar to familiars.

                    Yet I loved him
As one untainted by my shameful spells,
As one fit to be fledged – and then he flew!
How far and with what difficulty flew,
Far out beyond me, beyond that grey day
Far from our Dorset heath, our ambulations
Entranced with all my nurturings of talent,
Beyond the too-entrancing Cambridge courts
I lapsed towards, seeking again a brother . . .!

Dear brother in the outer room, you hear
A kind of trickling, a sound you cannot place:
That cold commemorator I encouraged
Will place it, use it, all grist for his mill.
I took the open razor to my throat.

Old pupil, you have new material now.

8　*A Message from Her*

I

So I dissembled: you dissembled too,
Striving to gain the fame you could not have.
You thought me your importunate young slave.
I thought you fierce to attain the things that you,
You only, could achieve. So we were wrong
In feigning each was only bent on each,
Eyes signalling to eyes, not needing speech.
The labour hence was tortuous and long,
Words broke to sentences, each phrase strung out
Like drunken men striving to stretch their thirst
Into the dawn, or lovers who at first
Believe each touch and kiss a final bout,
And then renewed, renewed . . . And each goes on
Battling, and feinting, reeling under blows
That deaden as the deadly feeling grows
That they are dead indeed; and dead and gone.

II

That gentle painter with beseeching eyes –
He was no menace: not the first, at least.
Some other bore the sign, mark of the beast,
Before he ever came. What sad surprise
When I escaped – more matter for your art!
This was the dizzy sickening of your will,
Sisyphus labouring up the stony hill,
Something that drained the nerves and pierced the heart:
An emptiness that gave me room to breathe
But vacuum to you – and how you strove,
Your lungs protesting, with what you used to love,
Your murderess . . . So our passions seethe,
Spill over, settle, chill. We learn to die
By living our own lives, leaving a room
Furnished like any self-respecting tomb,
The funeral bands disguising vacancy.

I left a note: 'He is in tears – I must
Go to him now.' And so the hours went by,
And you, of course, knew I could never lie.
But there I lay, lapped in an alien lust
That you could never understand, nor ever
Satisfy. Those broodings, those inert
And silent pangs that shadowed your sad hurt,
How could you contemplate what came to sever
Mismatched endurances with such a blow?
My love – my once love – you were far away,
Remembering some distant hallowed day
When from my gown I let the loose bands go
And I was Princess to your wandering Prince,
And all was fable, Land of Faery . . .
What you cast out, what you could never see –
That was the simple truth, long vanished since.

No word of me in letters, never a word
Let fall from that point onwards that I shared
Eight years with you, or that I ever cared
Concerning you. Fled like a migrant bird
To climes unknown, in ignorance I became
A footnote to your *opus*, quite cast out
Like the lean scapegoat who must bear the doubt
Because no other creature bears the blame.
And so I sickened – pitiless endless pain,
The swellings and the achings. Pale and weak,
I stumbled into debt, wrote letters, bleak
Day after day. For you, the deadly strain
Was not *my* dying but *your* distant fear
Of sickness and of death. I knew I must
Face on my own the test, accept the just
Reward for sin, and nowhere seek a tear.

V

How strange to be remembered in this way!
A set of almost-sonnets, crabbed yet rich,
Abrupt yet ample, stitch woven into stitch
As line by line you tell the present day
What happened, who kept silent, which one spoke
Words that must wound, how reverie went wrong,
And each verse carrying its bitter song –
Bitter, reproaching nothing but the yoke
That kept us bound together. This is how
Art will remember us, not in the ways
That stretched and broke us through those racking days
But in the mode that's apt and modish now:
Art for Art's sake . . . Forsaken, you set down
A set of tablets permanent as stone.
I was a wisp, a nothing, on my own,
Commemorated with an iron crown.

9 Seventy Years a Beggar

You think I'm drunk because my Irish voice
Is thick and crapulous – ah, there's a word
You wouldn't give me credit for: you think
I'm thick as peat, sir, thick as two short planks,
Because you hear my stumbling bumbling throat
Expectorate a load of roughened vowels.
Why smoothness, sir? Why should I learn to trim
Words that are mine to suit the vocables
That, polished, come from *your* mouth? I imbibed
Fine terms and cadences from all my tribe,
The Irish minstrelsy.

                    A crippled beggar
For forty years, a beggar before that
Since I could walk – my mother turned me out
To beg, because my father served the crown
In Egypt or some other foreign part
And never came back. I learned no trade. I might
Have learnt the shoemaking, but what's the use?
Fine times I had when the French war was on –
I lived in Westminster, one of two hundred
We called the Pye-Street Beggars, and our captain
Was Copenhagen Jack. Jack's word was law.
Each day he formed us up, gave us our beat:
'Twas share and share alike – the captain extra.
We had our lays – oh yes – the 'blind dodge darkies'
Who played at being blind, 'shakers' with fits,
And shipwrecked mariners who'd never seen the sea,
And men who took a bit of glass to scrape
Their feet until the blood ran – dodging lame, sir . . .

Not like my honest lameness. A horse and cart
Drove over me – well, yes, a trifle drunk, sir.
We lived like lords with Copenhagen Jack –
Fifty'd sit down to a supper, geese
And turkeys and all that, and keep it up
Till daylight with our songs and toasts.

                    Oh no,
There's nothing like it now: the new police
And this Mendicity Society has spoiled it all.
When Jack was 'pressed, his boys got rid of me –
They skinned me, took my coat and boots, turned out
In tatters on the 'orphan lay'. I cried
All day on the doorsteps, with my captain gone.
That won me ha'pence, though, and silver too,
And when I brought the swag home all the lads
Danced round and swore they'd make me captain next.
But when they'd had their fun, they took it all,
Kicked me under the table. I ran away,
Found a new house – St Giles – no captain there,
But better treatment. A hundred beggars,
Two or three hundred more in houses near –
Now all those houses gone, sir, taken down
When Oxford Street, New Oxford, was built up.
Oh we lived well then, St Giles and Westminster –
Eight, ten, fifteen, aye, thirty shillings a day
I've earned a-begging.

                        Not one shilling now.
The folks don't give today as they did then,
They think we're all impostures. And the police –
They won't let you alone. No, sir, I told you –
I never knew aught else but begging work:
How could I? 'Twas the trade I was brought up to.
A man must follow his trade. No doubt I'll die
A beggar, and the parish'll bury me.

A rum, sir? Thank you. And I'll speak you such
A ballad as my forebears left to me
From Holy Ireland. No, not drunk at all –
'Tis but my speech, a cockney Irish yet
The inheritance of kings, of bards, of saints,
Crippled, on crutches, with a tray of laces.

Pale beauties of a former day, lie there
Suppliant slaves attentive to my gaze!
My brush must worship you, large-eyed, bereft
Of all but wisps of gauze and feathered fans
In such a heat, the ancient classic sea
Glimpsed blue through the embrasure. How you strain
Mutely at these constraints I put on you,
Languid on couches, supine by the pool!

How different the view as now I turn
And look on dank back-gardens, dripping walls,
Façades of terraces, a distant spire,
And rank on rank of villas sprawling up
To crown this city fate has given me . . .
If I had been brought up among your groves,
Your temples and your chambers, purple-draped,
Sun-drenched in marble, what might I have been!

And so I use you, distant and ideal,
Maidens of modesty, passionate and still,
To be my paragons. My purposes
Are chaste, exact, sublime, and beautiful,
However men may misinterpret such
Voluptuous offerings – the upraised breasts,
The yearning thighs, the lips that, swollen, speak
Impulses we deny except to Art . . .

Back to the canvas . . . Think – in Manchester
My allegories grace those blackened fanes,
Suggesting a perspective we have spurned
In votes, and bills of lading, and machines
That knit and fret and petulantly stamp
Patterns on shoddiness, an endless wheel
Of usefulness and profit. Yet my shapes –
Lovingly nurtured, individual . . .

They say I make my profits too. 'Tis so –
I tug the heart, the lost inheritance,
And so the purse-strings. Is that shameful, then?
To please with what would else be lost to us?
They speak of *markets*: I am fortunate
In doing best what's best for my design,
Romantic ardour in a classic vein,
The pristine captured and brought down from heaven.

Watch how I mix the umber with the rose,
Tinctures of flesh beyond imaginings,
The dew still on the petal, light of light,
Waterdrops glistening on the lifted arm –
A talent, and a gift: no muddiness,
No crudity, no vaulting after vague
Resemblances, but everywhere my crisp
Edges of excellence, a bounding line.

These Frenchmen and these Dutch – I've heard of them,
But what about them? Vogues will come and go
As they have always done. The test must be
Standards established by the chosen few
Time has preserved for us – Praxiteles,
Phidias, a handful else. Where can Art go
Except in emulation? Here – the pink
Lies on the white, and trembles on the cheek.

Rich bronzes, figured vases, jewellery –
Fruits of my labours, subterranean joys:
My men sit round a dark sarcophagus,
Broken and plundered centuries ago,
And nod at noon. I sift and sift again,
Under the hottest sun, in longest hours
Of sleepy sweltering heat, intent on each
Small shovelful of soil, or sand, or ash.
No matter that the London functionaries
Hold back my proper monies, ignoring letters,
Museum men walled up in bills of lading,
Idly content that yet another consul
Should now and then transmit them treasures. Mine's
A nose for all that's oldest, finest, rarest,
From shy Etruscans to these desert shores
Where Battus first made landfall and the light
Of Greece first dawned in darkest Africa.
White-crowned Cyrene – never have I seen
A Grecian city so commanding, high
On its acropolis, with all around
A wilderness of tombs, deep lintelled caves,
Domes, and hog-backs, and noble architraves,
And hoarded grave-goods (even though despoilt
By brigands old and new) that catch the breath.

Not so this post my lords have given me –
A dreary town stuck betwixt sea and sand,
Salt-lakes, and hovels windowless and low
With stable-yard interiors like middens,
A crumbling castle, one poor minaret,
One grove of date palms, line after line of walls
Monotonously red, the houses unhewn stone
Bedded in mud, and rain, and filth, the whole
Wretched confusion a barbarity
Fit for the Barbary Shore . . . A tail-less lion
Over my doorway, in as quaint a style

As Mycenean, and a flag-staff – these
Alone distinguish my abode as that
Which represents Her Majesty. I hope
I am not doomed to a long exile here
In this *Ulubrae*, sand-girt, dead-dog-strewn.
Smyrna, Palermo – those I covet most . . .

Still, for the present I must grant it has
Greater attraction than it would possess
For many people: diggings established, soon
I hope to make a good haul of antiques.
As for my consular duties, I have borne
In mind your last injunction, that I should
Ingratiate myself among the Arabs. The other day
I visited a powerful tribe in camp –
Five or six hundred horsemen at a gallop,
Brandishing their long rifles, shouted welcome
And honoured me with races, firing muskets.
I am on good terms, also, with the Pasha:
I stood firm to his claims, and he withdrew
Pretentious interferences. I begin
To understand these oriental gentlemen –
I wish I could claim as much for what I know
Of their outlandish languages . . .

                              Many tombs,
Well-furnished I would guess, are even here
Hard by Benghazi, on the salt-lake shore.
More to the north-east, on the Tocra track,
Relieve the barren undulating waste,
Unfreshened by flower or shrub, by leaf or blade.
It is of these I wrote at the beginning,
The Tocra vases, finely beautiful,
Panathenaic some of them. Even more
The port of Apollonia presents
Far richer prizes, if I can persuade
A *firman* from the Pasha. Where I fear
Sole opposition is from the Brotherhoods,

The Convents of Senoussy who keep up
Fanaticism and intolerance
Among the lower Arabs: dangerous men.
Twice in my tour they threatened me with talk
Of 'Nazarene dog', and at Ptolmeita I
Escaped only because my *exequatur*
Displayed the Sultan's signature. Such trials
Do not, however, bring me to despair;
A spice of danger lends a certain relish
To searching for antiquities.

                    If Lord Somers
Should be inclined to pay this coast a visit,
I would delight to be his *cicerone*. Did I mention
At Apollonia the numerous columns
Of cipollino, relics of Christian churches,
To which the Turks attach no value, but
Which I am sure would be much prized in England,
Either perhaps to adorn the National Gallery
Or decorate the portico of a church?
May I beg the Admiral at Malta to allow
Some gunboat, on a cruise, to bear me hence
And lift these handsome spoils? Such prospects lighten
The burden of this wretchedness, the whines
Of Maltese litigants, the silences
I long endure from London. My dear Sir,
I beg you not to let me languish here,
Though I am avid for what treasures yet
May be vouchsafed to me.

Can these thick-pelted Calibans, deep in their dripping forests,
Be human as I am, or else collateral
Ancestors, the kin of apes and monkeys?
Such questions exercise the gentle reader
Snug in his study, holding in his armchair
My books of travel: they are not my questions.
Journeying, I best follow the old author –
Humani nil a me alienum puto.
For, from the moment England drops behind me
With all its rules of upbringing and habit,
Sensible tracts, quotidian drudgeries,
And all my dismal memories of girlhood,
I grow another face, become another person.

Travellers, indeed, are privileged to do
The most improper things imagined with
Perfect propriety. The sickly elder daughter
Whose youth was spent reclining on the sofas
In rectory drawing-rooms, with spinal trouble
That nagged through camomile and laudanum,
Now jolts on horseback through the wilderness,
Land of the Rising Sun's most northern island.

Evenings in plaited huts, gulping down rancid stews
(Boar offal, spongy roots, unnamable victuals),
Saké libations to the million deities
Worshipped in mountain, tree and rock and river,
Dim-lit interiors where elders endlessly
Spell out the genealogies of tribe and tribe,
And over all the mystery and the deluge
Descending like a revelation on me.
For God is here, among these (you say) savages,
As instrumental in his signs and wonders
As anywhere in tamer, temperate places.
No, I do not presume the evangelical:
My part is not the preaching of the Gospel,

Though some could only gauge what I am doing
In terms of carrying Bibles to the natives –
Aunt Mary as a missionary in India
Or Cousin Mary among Persian deserts.
These Ainu have no written law or history –
Indeed, no forms of written words among them –
And, placid in their sad, sweet resignation,
Only inflamed by copious potations
Of rice-wine spirits, are uncomprehending
At notions of a Saviour among them.

If you cast doubt upon the seemly wisdom
Of trusting female frailty to the dangers
Exposed by such benighted sole encounters,
I ask you, reader, merely to examine
Your storyteller as she stands before you:
Four-foot-eleven, a stumpy dumpy creature,
At her age – rising fifty – unencumbered
With fancies how her charms might be like tinder.
I trust myself to Ito, my interpreter –
Sharp-witted, vain and bandy-legged, a youth
Hot for his girls, his sweetmeats and his pride.
A foreign lady capable of 'drinking
To the gods' in their intoxicated fashion
Without intoxication, and whose questionings
Seek out the best and not the worst in all men –
They cannot harm me. Diligent and merry,
The grooms who take my horses and are humble
Could not depend entirely on the tardy
And insufficient efforts of the niggard
And selfish Church I grew in and grew up to.
God numbers these in his inheritance:
These heathens puzzled by the word 'salvation'
Will yet be saved – but not by my endeavours.
The gates of Heaven are wide and full of mercy,
Opening to all who follow in their fashion
The instincts they may never have acknowledged,
Whether Hawaii, Arkansas or Yorkshire

(Parishes known or unknown, known to me),
Loosed them to make their world their destiny.

Peevish I may be, briefly, at my portion
(I should have been a man, though would not say it
Except to Ito, who'll not understand),
But this I know – accept – embrace – and glory in –
The freedom of a journey that excuses
All things but cowardice, bad faith, incompetence,
And leaves me free to look at what was never
Revealed before to the sick English daughter
Of a good man who never could envisage
The stumbling trackways she can now exult in,
Far from the rooms she lay in once, alone.

Here, sir, a fine display of bravery
And fortitude, all rendered out of clay –
Here's Caius Mutius holding his right hand
Within the fire, showing Porsenna
The firmness of the Roman character;
On the reverse, the maid Cloelia
Selecting from the youthful hostages
Whom Porsenna will liberate. A piece
Noble and highly wrought, you will agree.
And by this vase, a terracotta plaque
Depicting in relief Da Vinci's great
'Battle of the Standard' – lavished round the rim
Oak leaves and acorns in the classic style.
This modelled wall-hanging won Second Prize
In 'Eighty-two at Braintree – Lucilus
Personates Brutus, an Old Master's work
Young Edward copied with a master's skill.
Glazed ornamental is our special pride,
Gem-ware encrusted, sprigged and polychrome –
But we love precedent in everything,
Old lessons handed on, the apostles' touch
Rendering all we make a sacrament
Blessed by the past – Egyptian, Roman, Greek,
Palissy plates and Babylonian shapes,
These ewers after Orazia Fontana's,
Tazzas adapted from Fijian ware
(Queen Emma of the Sandwich Isles came here,
And shook me by the hand, and bought a fine
Large model of our castle-keep, the source
Of so much inspiration – solid stuff,
Impregnable though ruined). Even these
Humbler creations have their ancestry:
Barm-pots and costrels, benisons and cloams,
Pottles and salt-kits, gallipots and tygs,
The rude plain earthenware, traditional instruments
Rustic amusement used, the puzzle-jugs,

The bird-whistles – I made them, one by one
And gross by gross, to stock the waggonloads
That left our workshop, sagging above wheels
Bedded in mud, for markets dwindling down
To half a dozen hawkers raucously
Shouting our old-style wares to new-style ears . . .

For that I fear's my story. What I put
In stone above the lintel is my text –
The psalmist's strong stern voice: 'Except the Lord
Do build the house, they labour in vain that build it' –
And vain the labour too. With sweating kilns
That marred whole bungs at firing, bubbles, bloats
Scarring the intricate sprays and sprigs and lugs,
Added to muddle casting-up accounts,
And sons who emigrated or who died,
And Fashion sniggering at our 'quaintnesses',
Grown fond of delicate mincing porcelain . . .
Fine feathering, tib-work, the antique ornate
Crossed with the sturdy native English style,
Slumped to mere jobbery, plain coarse flower-pots,
Nothings by anyone for anyone,
No individual stamp, no sense of that
Grandeur I gave a title to – 'Unique
Art Pottery Works of Castle Hedingham'
('The *Royal* Art', after Queen Emma's visit).
Zion bewails her pitiful estate,
'Esteemed as earthen pitchers' – meaning held
As low as dirt.
              And yet our dirt is *clay*,
Grog, slurry to be fashioned into lives
As vivid as the mud our Infant Lord
Shaped into sparrows from the gutter-side . . .

*

The grunting drays convey the crocks away
Where they will gather dust in crumbling sheds,

Back-ends of warehouses, a bankrupt's stock.
Here in my cottage by the castle wall
I slowly foot the treadle of the wheel
That turns the last ceramic I shall make
Before the vessel's broken and the sherds
Are thrown on to the spoil-heap where we lie
Until the angels' golden trumpets sound,
The Master Potter works his mystery,
And every fragment to its fragment's joined.

A dozen dogs, poodles and nondescripts,
My darlings barking at the iron gate . . .
Who might it be? There's no one left to call,
And so I sit useless, the garden wall
High as my disappointment, sit and wait
For the moths to eat away the innocence,
The honesty, the decency, and then
The whole new wardrobe I could not afford
From Worth – the vanity, the vain expense,
The flirting with Marchese and with Lord,
The opinionated converse with true men.

Now Robert Lytton's dead – a heart attack –
And della Stufa – cancer of the throat –
And Mario, too, whose voice enslaved me once –
All loves, all friendships, straitened and remote
As former fame, and flower-filled hotel rooms,
The Langham thirty years ago . . . Look askance,
You moralists who jib at genius,
At the pert message posted in the hall –
'Leave morals and umbrellas at the door'.
No invitation to reception, dance,
Wine, *conversazione*, concert, play,
For – what? – a dozen years . . . A villa, dank
And crumbling among cypresses, four floors,
Twenty-five rooms – myself and Gori stay
When Bagni drifts with leaves, and all have left.
Condemned to solitude, in poverty,
Furniture seized by creditors, bereft
Even of letters bundled over years,
Manuscripts auctioned, each royalty and fee
Reduced to farthings . . . No, these are not tears
But the dulled liquids of blue eyes that saw
Irving perform my gestures and my words.
Out of the world, my world, perhaps so much
The better, walled up here midst dogs and trees –

I am old, pathetic, angry, out of touch.
The world takes its revenge on us, because
We once despised it. Play it as you please,
Rewards must dwindle, style must go awry,
Voluptuousness grow vile, and Europe learn
The rage for slaughter. Middle-class spirits crush
The rapture and the passion of the soul,
Making it mute: thus Browning, Tennyson,
George Eliot – in chains, or chanting odes,
Or hypocritical in homilies.
Our genius is our spur, our passion goads
The highest from the best. Even in the tomb
The lustre shines like gold from sepulchres
Of lost Etruscan kings, or on the breast
Of some fair living woman, undimmed by dust,
The length of ages, or men's pettiness.

*

My dogs bark on among the cypress gloom,
A dozen Cerberuses whose yelps press
Hotly against the neglected effigy –
My own – where like a Florentine princess
I lie in Bagni, dead, unread, my name
A half-romantic joke, something to see
If tourists can be bothered to search out
A deaf custodian with a rusty key.
No flowers, no candles, no *frisson*-laden words
Await you there: the candles have gone out,
The flowers have faded, and the words are dull
As out-of-fashion dusty ballroom clothes
Hanging in wardrobes in deserted rooms.
The iron bell-handle's broken: when you pull,
The dogs grow hoarse not at the sound of it
But at the unfamiliar, painful smell
Which men call Life. And I am out of it.

Notes on Subjects and Sources

Most of these poems draw on actual individuals. It would be very nearly impossible to establish all the sources I have used, or for me to make a firm line between transcription and invention, but what follows is a list of the 'subjects' of the poems and an acknowledgement of those sources of which I am most conscious:

1. 'At Marychurch': Philip Henry Gosse (1810–1888). Gosse (the 'father' of Edmund Gosse's *Father and Son*) published his explanation of Creation, *Omphalos*, in 1857: Darwin, whom Gosse knew, published *The Origin of Species* in 1859. Marychurch, on the Devon coast, was where Gosse lived for over thirty years, and here he made many of his observations of marine biology.

2. 'A Literary Life': John Churton Collins (1848–1908). Collins was an industrious literary journalist and freelance lecturer who eventually held the first chair in English at Birmingham University. His attack on his old friend Edmund Gosse's Clark Lectures in the *Quarterly* was controversial, and earned a famous rebuke from Tennyson. His son, L. C. Collins, published the *Life and Memoirs of John Churton Collins* in 1912.

3. 'To a Girl of the Period': Eliza Lynn Linton (1822–1898). She married the engraver (and, in a mild way, bohemian social reformer) W. J. Linton, taking over his children by a former marriage, but was soon disillusioned and they separated. She was an indefatigable contributor to the periodicals, chiefly of essays on 'the new woman', and in particular of a group later collected and published as *The Girl of the Period and other Social Essays* (1883). George Somes Layard published *Mrs Lynn Linton: Her Life, Letters and Opinions* in 1901.

4. 'Messages from Government House': James Ramsay, Marquess of Dalhousie (1812–1860). He became Governor-General of India in 1848, and left India in 1856 before the Mutiny the following year. The *Private Letters of the Marquess of Dalhousie* were edited by J. G. A. Bair in 1910.

5. 'Parables from Nature': Margaret Gatty (1809–1873). A prolific writer for children, she was married to an Anglican clergyman, the Rev. Alfred Gatty. Her *Parables from Nature* appeared in 1896 with a memoir by her daughter, Juliana Horatia Ewing, also a notable children's writer.

6. 'After High Table': an amalgam and/or invention, drawing on several hints in (among other places) Jan Morris's *Oxford Book of Oxford* (1978) and Mark Pattison's *Memoirs* (1885). I imagine an elderly don in the 1860s and 1870s, ordained, but in many ways a survival from a period less given to religious searching and debate.

7. 'The Mentor': Horace Moule (1832–1873). Moule came from a family of respectable dons and clerics, and had hopes of becoming a scholar and literary man. In 1857 he befriended the young Thomas Hardy, who later made use of him in *Jude the Obscure* and several poems. Moule was said to have got a village girl pregnant: the son of this union was later hanged in Australia. Moule killed himself in his brother's rooms in Cambridge. See *Young Thomas Hardy* by Robert Gittings (1975).

8. 'A Message from Her': Mary Ellen Meredith (1821–1861). She was the daughter of Thomas Love Peacock, and married George Meredith in 1849. After eight years of unhappiness, she left with the painter Henry Wallis, but died in 1861, alone and after much illness. Meredith's sequence of 16-line poems, *Modern Love*, is in part based on their marriage. A standard source for the story is Siegfried Sassoon's life of Meredith (1948); a much more biased account is Diane Johnson's *Lesser Lives* (1972), but it has the advantage of drawing on some hitherto unpublished material.

41

9. 'Seventy Years a Beggar': see Henry Mayhew's *London Labour and the London Poor*, Volume Four, 1864. The beggar is based on one of the people interviewed by Mayhew for this pioneering work of sociology (or investigative journalism).

10. 'The Studio': loosely based on Lawrence Alma-Tadema (1836–1912). Alma-Tadema's best-known paintings are neo-classical studies, such as 'In the Tepidarium'. His work was technically adept, erotic in a subdued mode, and fashionable in its day.

11. 'The Consul at Benghazi': George Dennis (1814–1898). Dennis combined civil service and consular duties with a passion for antiquarianism, first in Italy (where he made some considerable researches into the Etruscans), then in Benghazi between 1864 and 1868. D. E. Rhodes published *Dennis of Etruria* in 1973; in spite of its title, the book also covers the later period of Dennis's life, including the Benghazi years.

12. 'On Horseback through Hokkaido': Isabella Bird (1831–1904). She was the delicate daughter of a Yorkshire clergyman, but in time became an intrepid traveller in many parts of the world. She published *Unbeaten Tracks in Japan* in 1880. Pat Barr published a delightful biography of her, *A Curious Life for a Lady*, in 1970.

13. 'The Potter's Field': Edward Bingham (1829–190?). Bingham's father founded the Castle Hedingham Pottery in Essex in 1837. Edward Bingham specialized in extraordinarily fanciful – and frequently ugly – variations on medieval earthenware, mixed with a widely eclectic range of other styles. He was a devout and fervent Evangelical. The standard study is *The Story of Castle Hedingham Pottery* by R. J. Bradley (1968); in the same year Bevis Hillier published his *Pottery and Porcelain, 1700–1914*, which contains a good brief account of Bingham and his work.

14. 'From the Villa Massoni': 'Ouida' (Louisa Ramé, 1839–1909). Between 1861 and 1867, Ouida published the astonishing number of forty-seven books, many of which (in particular *Under Two Flags*) were very successful. Exhausted by such productivity, she travelled to Florence to recuperate, and spent almost the whole of the rest of her life in Italy. In 1895 she moved with her faithful maid Gori to the Villa Massoni at Bagni di Lucca, by which time her literary reputation was in eclipse. Her effigy, deliberately imitating the style of della Quercia's statue of Ilaria del Carretto in the Duomo at Lucca, is in the Protestant Cemetery at Bagni. Ouida's *Views and Opinions* were published in 1895. Another useful source was *Paradise of Exiles* by Olive Hamilton (1974).

I should also like to thank the following for suggestions and sympathetic interest: Alistair Elliot, Ronald Ewart, Roy Fuller, Patricia Hollis, Rosemary Jackson, Peter Porter, my mother and my wife.